Print Handwriting Workbook for Adults

Advanced Print Handwriting Worksheets with Intriguing Historical Facts for a Meaningful Practice

Introduction to Advanced Print Handwriting

The goal of this workbook is to help you improve your print handwriting skills to an advanced level. It contains exercises for rewriting entire paragraphs and sentences. The font size is smaller compared to other standard children's practice worksheets.

This book also contains a short practice section for each letter. I recommend you complete this section first and practice each letter, before moving to the actual exercises. This section also includes recommendations on how each letter should be written. The rest of the workbook contains intriguing historical facts about ancient civilizations like:

- *Ancient Greece*
- *Ancient Persia*
- *Ancient Rome*
- *Ancient Egypt*
- *Ancient China*

At the beginning of each worksheet, you will find the historical fact written in a traceable font, after that you should use the remaining space to rewrite the entire fact again.

While I believe that everyone should know how to write in cursive. Print handwriting doesn't go without its merits. It can help you develop a more structured and legible writing style. It is therefore important in our modern society to master both cursive and print handwriting styles. This workbook focuses on the latter.

In order to obtain the most value out of this workbook, you should not only practice your print handwriting but also improve your knowledge by learning from the historical facts presented in this book. These facts can offer you meaningful insight into our cultures of origin as well as cultures which might be less familiar to you.

Print uppercase letters

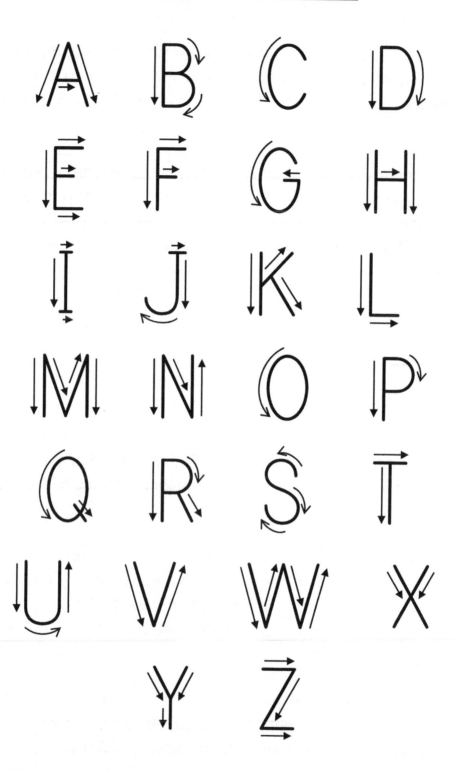

Print lowercase letters

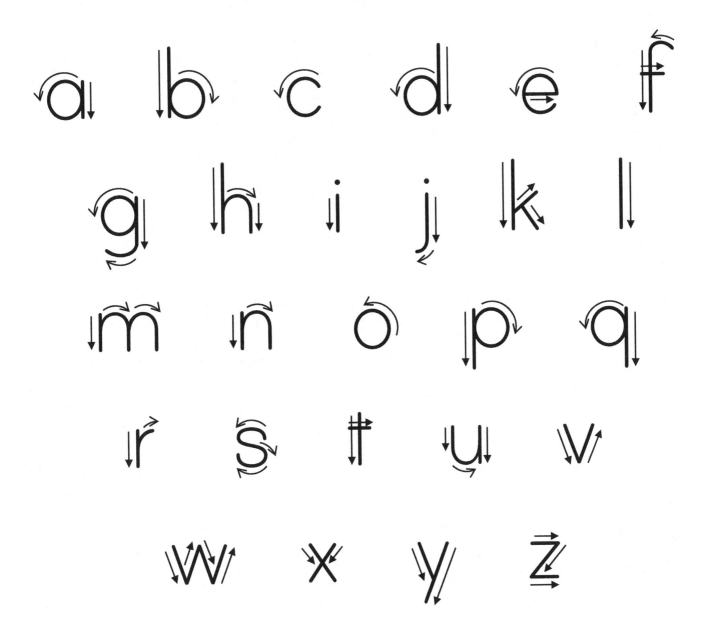

Print letter practice

A

a

B

b

C

c

D

d

E

e

F

f

G

g

H

h

I

j

J

j

K

k

L

l

M

m

N

n

O

O

P

O

Q

q

R

r

S

s

I

t

U

u

V

v

W

W

X

X

Y

Y

Z

Z

Historical Fact No.1 – Ancient Greece
It's believed that the Myceneans of Crete formed the first Ancient Greek civilizations approximately 4000 years ago.

It's believed that the

Myceneans of Crete formed

the first Ancient Greek

civilizations approximately

4000 years ago.

Historical Fact No.2 - Ancient Greece

The ancient Greeks believed that beans contained the souls of the dead and for that reason, they would refuse to eat them.

The ancient Greeks believed
that beans contained the
souls of the dead and for
that reason, they would
refuse to eat them.

Historical Fact No.3 – Ancient Greece

The world's first democracy was introduced in ancient Greece and lasted for 185 years.

The world's first democracy
was introduced in ancient
Greece and lasted for 185
years.

Historical Fact No.4 – Ancient Greece

Some of the most famous mythological creatures stemmed from Greek mythology, including the Cerberus, Medusa and the Cyclops.

Some of the most famous
mythological creatures
stemmed from Greek
mythology, including the
Cerberus, Medusa and the
Cyclops.

Historical Fact No.5 – Ancient Greece

Ancient Greece once had the most advanced economy in the world (between the 5th and 4th century BC).

Ancient Greece once had
the most advanced economy
in the world (between the
5th and 4th century BC).

Historical Fact No.6 – Ancient Greece

Ancient Athenian boys were sent to school at the age of 7, however, Spartan boys of the same age were taken and trained as soldiers.

Ancient Athenian boys were
sent to school at the age of
7, however, Spartan boys of
the same age were taken
and trained as soldiers.

Historical Fact No.7 – Ancient Greece

Spartan soldiers were not allowed to live with their families until they were 30 years old, when they could leave the military service.

Spartan soldiers were not
allowed to live with their
families until they were 30
years old, when they could
leave the military service.

Historical Fact No.8 - Ancient Greece

Ancient Greeks believed in zombies and took measures to ensure the dead would not rise from their graves.

Ancient Greeks believed in
zombies and took measures
to ensure the dead would not
rise from their graves.

Historical Fact No.9 – Ancient Greece

The ancient Olympic Games took place in honor of Zeus, the father of the Greek gods and goddesses. This event was, therefore, considered a religious event as much as it was an athletic one.

The ancient Olympic Games
took place in honor of Zeus,
the father of the Greek gods
and goddesses. This event
was, therefore, considered a
religious event as much as it
was an athletic one.

Historical Fact No.10 – Ancient Greece

Although the Greek city-states were often at war, a truce was called in the month before the Olympic Games so that spectators could safely travel to Olympia.

Although the Greek city-states
were often at war, a truce
was called in the month
before the Olympic Games so
that spectators could safely
travel to Olympia.

Historical Fact No.11 – Ancient Greece

The first alarm clock was invented around the
4th century BC by the Greek philosopher Plato.

The first alarm clock was
invented around the 4th
century BC by the Greek
philosopher Plato.

Historical Fact No.12 – Ancient Greece

The Battle of Salamis is considered to be one of the most significant battles in human history. It was a naval battle fought in 480 BC between an alliance of Greek city-states and the Persian Empire under King Xerxes. A Persian victory would have changed Western civilization as we know it today.

The Battle of Salamis is
considered to be one of the
most significant battles in
human history. It was a naval
battle fought in 480 BC
between an alliance of Greek
city-states and the Persian
Empire under King Xerxes. A
Persian victory would have
changed Western civilization
as we know it today

Historical Fact No.13 – Ancient Greece

Alexander the Great became king following his father's death in 336 BC. During his kingship, he managed to conquer most of the world known to the ancient Greeks.

Alexander the Great became
king following his father's
death in 336 BC. During his
kingship, he managed to
conquer most of the world
known to the ancient Greeks

Historical Fact No.14 – Ancient Greece

During the Pyrrhic war, between 280-275 BC, the Greeks used war elephants against the Romans.

During the Pyrrhic war,
between 280-275 BC, the
Greeks used war elephants
against the Romans.

Historical Fact No.15 – Ancient Greece

The Romans took control of the Greek peninsula
after the battle of Corinth in 146 BC.

The Romans took control of
the Greek peninsula after the
battle of Corinth in 146 BC.

Historical Fact No.16 – Ancient Persia

The Persian Empire started as a collection of semi-nomadic tribes who raised sheep, goats and cattle on the Iranian plateau.

The Persian Empire started as a collection of semi-nomadic tribes who raised sheep, goats and cattle on the Iranian plateau.

Historical Fact No.17 – Ancient Persia

Cyrus the Great founded the first Persian Empire, also known as the Achaemenid Empire, in 550 BC.

Cyrus the Great founded the
first Persian Empire, also
known as the Achaemenid
Empire, in 550 BC.

Historical Fact No.18 – Ancient Persia

Under the rule of King Cyrus the Great, the Persians created the first human rights charter.

Under the rule of King Cyrus
the Great, the Persians
created the first human rights
charter.

Historical Fact No.19 – Ancient Persia

During the reign of Cyrus the Great, the Persians allowed the people they conquered to continue their lives and cultures. This meant that they could keep their traditions and religions, as long as they obeyed the Persian rules and paid their taxes.

During the reign of Cyrus the
Great, the Persians allowed
the people they conquered
to continue their lives and
cultures. This meant that they
could keep their traditions
and religions, as long as they
obeyed the Persian rules and
paid their taxes.

Historical Fact No.20 – Ancient Persia

In order to maintain control over the entire Persian Empire, each area had a ruler called a satrap.

In order to maintain control
over the entire Persian Empire,
each area had a ruler called a
satrap.

Historical Fact No.21 – Ancient Persia

The Persians were also the first people to introduce
regular routes of communication between Africa,
Asia and Europe.

The Persians were also the

first people to introduce

regular routes of

communication between

Africa, Asia and Europe.

Historical Fact No.22 – Ancient Persia

In Ancient Persia, the first postal system was developed in Assyria between 550 BC and 521 BC.

In Ancient Persia, the first
postal system was developed
in Assyria between 550 BC
and 521 BC.

Historical Fact No.23 – Ancient Persia

At the height of its power, the Persian Empire covered everything from Europe's Balkan Peninsula to the Indus River Valley in northwest India and south to Egypt.

At the height of its power,
the Persian Empire covered
everything from Europe's
Balkan Peninsula to the Indus
River Valley in northwest India
and south to Egypt

The ceremonial capital of the Persian Empire was the city of Persepolis.

The ceremonial capital of the

Persian Empire was the city

of Persepolis.

Historical Fact No.25 – Ancient Persia

The Persian Empire was heavily influenced by a religion called Zoroastrianism.

The Persian Empire was heavily
influenced by a religion called
Zoroastrianism.

Historical Fact No.26 – Ancient Persia

Zoroastrianism was named after the Persian prophet called Zoroaster. He was one of the first who taught his followers to worship one god: Ahura Mazda.

Zoroastrianism was named
after the Persian prophet
called Zoroaster. He was one
of the first who taught his
followers to worship one god:
Ahura Mazda.

Historical Fact No.27 – Ancient Persia

The longest reigning Persian King was Artaxerxes II, who ruled for 45 years. His reign was a time of peace and prosperity for the Achaemenid empire.

The longest reigning Persian
King was Artaxerxes II, who
ruled for 45 years. His reign
was a time of peace and
prosperity for the Achaemenid
empire.

Historical Fact No.28 – Ancient Persia

At the height of its power, the Persian Empire had a population of 50 million. At that time, this represented approximately 44% of the world's entire population.

At the height of its power,
the Persian Empire had a
population of 50 million. At
that time, this represented
approximately 44% of the
world's entire population.

Historical Fact No.29 – Ancient Persia

Persian emperors demanded total obedience from their subjects. In order to enforce this message, they called themselves "The King of Kings".

Persian emperors demanded
total obedience from their
subjects. In order to enforce
this message, they called
themselves "The King of
Kings"

Historical Fact No.30 – Ancient Persia

In the Persian culture, lying was considered to be one of the most disgraceful acts a person could commit.

In the Persian culture, lying
was considered to be one of
the most disgraceful acts a
person could commit.

Historical Fact No.31 – Ancient Persia

The Persian Empire had an elite infantry of 10,000 men called "The Immortals". They were heavily armed and performed the roles of both imperial guard and standing army.

The Persian Empire had an
elite infantry of 10,000 men
called "The Immortals". They
were heavily armed and
performed the roles of both
imperial guard and standing
army.

Historical Fact No.32 – Ancient Persia

Ancient Persia founded the first teaching hospital in Gundishapur. There, medical students would practice on patients while supervised.

Ancient Persia founded the

first teaching hospital in

Gundishapur. There, medical

students would practice on

patients while supervised.

Historical Fact No.33 – Ancient Persia

After the failed invasion of Greece by Xerxes in 480 BC, the Persian Empire entered into a period of decline.

After the failed invasion of
Greece by Xerxes in 480 BC,
the Persian Empire entered
into a period of decline.

Historical Fact No.34 – Ancient Persia

In 330 BC, the Persian Empire fell under the invading armies of Alexander the Great.

In 330 BC, the Persian Empire
fell under the invading armies
of Alexander the Great.

Historical Fact No.35 – Ancient Rome

The ancient Roman Civilization started during the 8th century BC on the Italian Peninsula.

The ancient Roman Civilization
started during the 8th century
BC on the Italian Peninsula.

Historical Fact No.36 – Ancient Rome

Roman legend says that Romulus, the founder of the Roman civilization, had a twin brother named Remus. They were both abandoned as babies and raised by a she-wolf. It's said that in later years, Romulus fought and defeated Remus and became the first ruler of Rome.

Roman legend says that
Romulus, the founder of the
Roman civilization, had a twin
brother named Remus. They
were both abandoned as
babies and raised by a she-
wolf. It's said that in later
years, Romulus fought and
defeated Remus and became
the first ruler of Rome.

Historical Fact No.37 – Ancient Rome

Rome had 7 kings before it became a republic. The last king was deposed by Lucius Junius Brutus in 509 BC.

Rome had 7 kings before it
became a republic. The last
king was deposed by Lucius
Junius Brutus in 509 BC.

Historical Fact No.38 – Ancient Rome

Gaius Julius Caesar was born in the year 100 BC.

Gaius Julius Caesar was born in the year 100 BC.

Historical Fact No.39 — Ancient Rome

After Julius Caesar was forced to go into hiding due to
his father's death, he was kidnapped by pirates while
crossing the Aegean Sea.

After Julius Caesar was
forced to go into hiding due
to his father's death, he was
kidnapped by pirates while
crossing the Aegean Sea.

Historical Fact No.40 – Ancient Rome

Caesar started a civil war in 50 BC by crossing the Rubicon River into northern Italy.

Caesar started a civil war in
50 BC by crossing the Rubicon
River into northern Italy

Historical Fact No.41 – Ancient Rome

Julius Caesar was killed on 15th March by a group
of 60 men.

Julius Caesar was killed on

15th March by a group of 60

men.

Historical Fact No.42 – Ancient Rome

The Roman Empire was founded in 27 BC, when Augustus Caesar became the first emperor of Rome.

The Roman Empire was
founded in 27 BC, when
Augustus Caesar became the
first emperor of Rome.

Historical Fact No.43 – Ancient Rome

At the height of its power, the Roman Empire comprised the whole of Italy, all the lands located around the Mediterranean Sea and much of Europe.

At the height of its power,

the Roman Empire comprised

the whole of Italy, all the

lands located around the

Mediterranean Sea and much

of Europe.

Historical Fact No.44 – Ancient Rome

The Roman Empire owes its success largely to its strong army. The Roman army could walk up to 40 km in a single day.

The Roman Empire owes its
success largely to its strong
army. The Roman army could
walk up to 40 km in a single
day.

Historical Fact No.45 – Ancient Rome

The life expectancy in ancient Rome was only around 20-30 years old.

The life expectancy in ancient
Rome was only around 20-30
years old.

Historical Fact No.46 – Ancient Rome

The Roman Empire was only the 28th largest Empire in the world. Even at its peak, it contained just 12% of the world's population.

The Roman Empire was only
the 28th largest Empire in the
world. Even at its peak, it
contained just 12% of the
world's population.

Historical Fact No.47 – Ancient Rome

The Romans were not only good at fighting, they were also excellent engineers and architects. Their inventions inspired the world for centuries to come.

The Romans were not only
good at fighting, they were
also excellent engineers and
architects. Their inventions
inspired the world for
centuries to come.

Historical Fact No.48 – Ancient Rome

The Persian-Roman wars lasted for approximately 700 years.

The Persian-Roman wars

lasted for approximately 700

years.

Historical Fact No.49 – Ancient Rome

Saturnalia was an ancient Roman festival during which the master and his slaves would switch places. It was held in honor of the deity Saturn.

Saturnalia was an ancient

Roman festival during which

the master and his slaves

would switch places. It was

held in honor of the deity

Saturn.

Historical Fact No.50 – Ancient Rome

The most common item of Roman clothing was the tunic. These consisted of two pieces of woolen fabric sewn together, with openings for the arms and head.

The most common item of

Roman clothing was the tunic.

These consisted of two

pieces of woolen fabric sewn

together, with openings for

the arms and head.

Historical Fact No.51 – Ancient Rome

During the reign of the Roman Empire, Paris was a
Roman city called Lutetia.

During the reign of the Roman
Empire, Paris was a Roman
city called Lutetia.

Historical Fact No.52 – Ancient Rome

Roman soldiers were partially paid in salt. During those times, salt was scarce and considered an expensive commodity.

Roman soldiers were partially
paid in salt. During those
times, salt was scarce and
considered an expensive
commodity.

Historical Fact No.53 – Ancient Rome

The Romans used to flood the entire Colosseum in order to perform mock sea battles.

The Romans used to flood the entire Colosseum in order to perform mock sea battles.

Historical Fact No.54 – Ancient Rome

The Roman Empire reached its greatest geographical extent during the reign of Trajan (98 – 117 AD). During that time, it covered around 5 million square km.

The Roman Empire reached its
greatest geographical extent
during the reign of Trajan (98
– 117 AD). During that time, it
covered around 5 million
square km.

Historical Fact No.55 – Ancient Egypt

Ancient Egyptians worshipped more than 1000 gods and goddesses.

Ancient Egyptians worshipped more than 1000 gods and goddesses.

Historical Fact No.56 – Ancient Egypt

Ancient Egyptians performed the mummification process because they believed that in order for the dead to be reborn in the afterlife, the body needed to be preserved.

Ancient Egyptians performed
the mummification process
because they believed that in
order for the dead to be
reborn in the afterlife, the
body needed to be preserved.

Historical Fact No.57 – Ancient Egypt

Egyptian animals were also mummified. They were viewed not only as pets, but also as incarnations of gods.

Egyptian animals were also
mummified. They were viewed
not only as pets, but also as
incarnations of gods.

Historical Fact No.58 – Ancient Egypt

Since the mummification process took so long and had to be performed by embalmers, the majority of regular citizens were just buried in shallow graves with their belongings.

Since the mummification

process took so long and had

to be performed by

embalmers, the majority of

regular citizens were just

buried in shallow graves with

their belongings.

Historical Fact No.59 – Ancient Egypt

Carving hieroglyphs was extremely time-consuming and therefore reserved only for the most important texts and spells.

Carving hieroglyphs was
extremely time-consuming and
therefore reserved only for
the most important texts and
spells.

Historical Fact No.60 – Ancient Egypt

The oldest dress ever found was worn in Ancient Egypt.
It is known as the Tarkhan dress and was made of linen.
This dress is over 5000 years old.

The oldest dress ever found
was worn in Ancient Egypt. It
is known as the Tarkhan dress
and was made of linen. This
dress is over 5000 years old.

Historical Fact No.61 – Ancient Egypt

The youngest pharaoh to rule in Ancient Egypt was Tutankhamun.

The youngest pharaoh to rule
in Ancient Egypt was
Tutankhamun.

Historical Fact No.62 – Ancient Egypt

Contrary to popular belief, the pyramids were not built by slaves but by hired workers. Building the pyramids for the pharaohs was considered to be a great honor.

Contrary to popular belief, the
pyramids were not built by
slaves but by hired workers.
Building the pyramids for the
pharaohs was considered to
be a great honor.

Historical Fact No.63 – Ancient Egypt

Beer was an important part of Ancient Egyptian society. So important, in fact, that they even worshipped a goddess of beer known as Tjenenet.

Beer was an important part of
Ancient Egyptian society. So
important, in fact, that they
even worshipped a goddess
of beer known as Tjenenet.

Historical Fact No.64 – Ancient Egypt

In Ancient Egypt, both men and women used to wear makeup on a regular basis.

In Ancient Egypt, both men
and women used to wear
makeup on a regular basis.

Historical Fact No.65 – Ancient Egypt

The Ancient Egyptians discovered a way to keep the temperature inside the pyramids at a constant level of 20 degrees Celsius.

The Ancient Egyptians
discovered a way to keep the
temperature inside the
pyramids at a constant level
of 20 degrees Celsius.

Historical Fact No.66 – Ancient Egypt

One of the most famous Egyptian symbols, which is still used to this day, is the Eye of Horus. It represents royal power, protection, and good health.

One of the most famous
Egyptian symbols, which is
still used to this day, is the
Eye of Horus. It represents
royal power, protection, and
good health.

Historical Fact No.67 – Ancient Egypt

It is believed that Ancient Egyptian women had equal rights to men.

It is believed that Ancient
Egyptian women had equal
rights to men.

Historical Fact No.68 – Ancient Egypt

Even though Egyptian rulers were depicted as athletic and slim, it is believed that most of them were obese and lived an unhealthy lifestyle.

Even though Egyptian rulers
were depicted as athletic and
slim, it is believed that most
of them were obese and lived
an unhealthy lifestyle.

Historical Fact No.69 – Ancient Egypt

The civilization of Ancient Egypt lasted over
3000 years, from 3150 BC to 30 BC.

The civilization of Ancient
Egypt lasted over 3000 years,
from 3150 BC to 30 BC.

Historical Fact No.70 – Ancient Egypt

Some of the most common household items, such as toothpaste, paper, keys and locks, were invented in Ancient Egypt.

Some of the most common
household items, such as
toothpaste, paper, keys and
locks, were invented in
Ancient Egypt.

Historical Fact No.71 – Ancient Egypt

Cleopatra was actually a descendant of Greek Macedonians.

Cleopatra was actually a descendant of Greek Macedonians.

Historical Fact No.72 – Ancient Egypt

The statue of the Sphinx was built to guard the pyramid of Khafre at Giza.

The statue of the Sphinx was
built to guard the pyramid of
Khafre at Giza.

Historical Fact No.73 – Ancient China

The first Chinese emperor was Shi Huangdi. After his death, his second oldest son forged a letter stating that the eldest must commit suicide so that he would become emperor. The plan worked.

The first Chinese emperor was Shi Huangdi. After his death, his second eldest son forged a letter stating that the eldest must commit suicide so that he would become emperor. The plan worked.

Historical Fact No.74 - Ancient China

Legend says that the Chinese Goddess, Nu Gua, created humanity because she did not want the Yellow River to stay quiet and alone.

Legend says that the Chinese Goddess, Nu Gua, created humanity because she did not want the Yellow River to stay quiet and alone.

Historical Fact No.75 – Ancient China

The Great Wall of China was first built in segments by ancient Chinese states. Later on, the walls were joined together during the Qin Dynasty by the first Emperor of China.

The Great Wall of China was
first built in segments by
ancient Chinese states. Later
on, the walls were joined
together during the Qin
Dynasty by the first Emperor
of China.

Historical Fact No.76 – Ancient China

The Great Wall of China was primarily built to protect the Chinese Empire from the Mongolians and other invaders.

The Great Wall of China was
primarily built to protect the
Chinese Empire from the
Mongolians and other invaders

Historical Fact No.77 – Ancient China

Yu the Great was considered an extraordinary ruler by the ancient Chinese. He introduced flood control and established the Xia Dynasty.

Yu the Great was considered
an extraordinary ruler by the
ancient Chinese He introduced
flood control and established
the Xia Dynasty.

Historical Fact No.78 – Ancient China

The only empress of China was Wu Zetian. She was the wife of two different emperors and rose to power by usurping the throne.

The only empress of China

was Wu Zetian. She was the

wife of two different

emperors and rose to power

by usurping the throne.

Historical Fact No.79 – Ancient China

During the Qing Dynasty, Emperor Qianlong was able to cancel taxes due to the imperial treasury being too full.

During the Qing Dynasty,
Emperor Qianlong was able
to cancel taxes due to the
imperial treasury being too
full.

Historical Fact No.80 – Ancient China

Xiang Yu burned all of his ships and cooking gear the night before attacking the Qin Dynasty. This was so that his army would have no other option but to win or else perish.

Xiang Yu burned all of his
ships and cooking gear the
night before attacking the Qin
Dynasty. This was so that his
army would have no other
option but to win or else
perish.

Historical Fact No.81 – Ancient China

During the Zhou dynasty, several Chinese kingdoms used knives as currency more than they did coins.

During the Zhou dynasty,
several Chinese kingdoms
used knives as currency more
than they did coins.

Historical Fact No.82 – Ancient China

In Ancient China, the lotus was considered a symbol of purity.

In Ancient China, the lotus was considered a symbol of purity.

Historical Fact No.83 – Ancient China

The ancient Chinese invented kites, fireworks and gunpowder.

The ancient Chinese invented kites, fireworks and gunpowder.

Historical Fact No.84 – Ancient China

The Zhou Dynasty was the longest ruling dynasty in China's history. It ruled from 1046 to 256 BC.

The Zhou Dynasty was the
longest ruling dynasty in
China's history. It ruled from
1046 to 256 BC.

Historical Fact No.85 – Ancient China

Puyi was the last Emperor of China. He became the ruler when he was only three years old.

Puyi was the last Emperor of
China. He became the ruler
when he was only three years
old.

Historical Fact No.86 – Ancient China

The dragon was used by Emperors in China as a symbol of power, strength and good luck.

The dragon was used by
Emperors in China as a symbol
of power, strength and good
luck.

Historical Fact No.87 – Ancient China

The first people to drink tea for medicinal purposes were the ancient Chinese.

The first people to drink tea
for medicinal purposes were
the ancient Chinese.

Historical Fact No.88 – Ancient China

The Oracle Bone Calendar was the first known Chinese calendar, dating back to 1200 BC.

The Oracle Bone Calendar was
the first known Chinese
calendar, dating back to
1200 BC.

Historical Fact No.89 – Ancient China

The three main Chinese religions were Daoism,
Buddhism and Confucianism.

The three main Chinese
religions were Daoism,
Buddhism and Confucianism.

Historical Fact No.90 — Ancient China

Before paper itself was invented, bamboo strips
were used by ancient Chinese writers.

Before paper itself was
invented, bamboo strips were
used by ancient Chinese
writers.

Historical Fact No.91 – Ancient China

Under the Shang Dynasty, entire families were required to participate in military operations in case of war.

Under the Shang Dynasty,
entire families were required
to participate in military
operations in case of war.

Historical Fact No.92 — Ancient China

Giant pandas, which were considered a symbol of bravery, existed in China as far back as two to three million years ago.

Giant pandas, which were
considered a symbol of
bravery, existed in China as
far back as two to three
million years ago.

Historical Fact No.93 – Ancient China

People who visited the Royal Court were expected to kneel and tap their forehead on the ground nine times. This was supposed to signify respect to their ruler.

People who visited the Royal
Court were expected to kneel
and tap their forehead on the
ground nine times. This was
supposed to signify respect
to their ruler.

Historical Fact No.94 – Ancient China

Due to his fear of being killed, Emperor Shih Huang-Ti built a network of 270 palaces and slept in a different one every night.

Due to his fear of being
killed, Emperor Shih Huang-Ti
built a network of 270 palaces
and slept in a different one
every night.

91728802R00057